IMAGES OF

HAMPSHIRE

AND THE NEW FOREST

Terry Heathcote

HALSGROVE

First published in 1999 by Halsgrove

ISBN 1 84114 022 8

British Library Cataloguing-in-Publication-Data
A CIP data record for this book is available from the British Library

HALSGROVE
Halsgrove House
Lower Moor Way
Tiverton EX16 6SS
T: 01884 243242
F: 01884 243325
e-mail: sales@halsgrove.com

Printed and bound in Singapore by
UIC Printing and Packaging Pte Ltd

CONTENTS

BASINGSTOKE, AND THE NORTHERN BORDER
ANDOVER, WHITCHURCH AND THE UPPER TEST
STOCKBRIDGE, ROMSEY AND THE LOWER TEST
WINCHESTER AND THE CENTRAL CHALKLANDS
ALTON, PETERSFIELD AND THE WESTERN WEALD
SOUTHAMPTON AND SOUTHAMPTON WATER
PORTSMOUTH, FAREHAM AND THE MEON VALLEY
THE NEW FOREST AND THE SOUTH WEST COAST
The Solent

INTRODUCTION

There can be few, if any, counties to match the sheer range of interest and scenery, both natural and man-made, provided by Hampshire, and even fewer that provide such continuity of history over the centuries. In many ways the county could be said to encapsulate the very essence of England and Englishness.

At its heart is Winchester, the county town and once capital of England where, in the tranquil confines of the cathedral, will be found memorials to former kings such as Canute and William the First, conqueror of England.

To the north is Basingstoke, now nearly lost to modern development and, nearby, Old Basing, the site of such horrors during the Civil War. The grandeur of Highclere Castle, heathlands of Yateley Common and impressive remains of the once great Roman town of Calleva Atrebetum at Silchester will all be found along these lesser known northern borders.

The attractive market towns of Alton and Petersfield, both surrounded by beautiful scenery, are found to the east of the county. The steep hangers, sunken lanes and sweeping downland of this area were familiar to Gilbert White, the famous naturalist. Further to the south the string of villages along the Meon Valley are equally attractive although set among somewhat less dramatic scenery.

Rising in Ashe is the River Test, world renowned for its trout fishing and dominating the western side of the county. By-passing Andover, an ancient town which still retains its market despite recent developments, the river meanders south until eventually reaching Southampton Water. Along its course are found tiny villages which have changed little over the centuries, and small market towns such as Stockbridge with its single wide street bridging the river and Romsey, lying in the shadow of the great abbey church.

The south coast of Hampshire supports the greater part of the population, yet even here a rich history survives and, in parts, lonely beauty as well.

Ships reflecting the glory of years long past are found in the historic dockyard of Portsmouth standing cheek by jowl with warships of the modern navy. Nearby and in complete contrast is the peaceful haven of Langstone Harbour, internationally known for its wealth of bird life. Along the coast, beyond the faded glory of Netley Abbey, is Southampton. Even here, with its thriving town centre and newly emerging shopping development, said to be the largest in Europe, many parts of the medieval town remain. The old town walls are much in evidence including the West Gate where the pilgrims departed on their brave journey to America. Today the great ocean liners are again plying their trade from the busy docks, whilst ever increasing numbers of yachtsmen continue to enjoy the challenge of the Solent.

Tucked away in the south-west corner between Southampton Water and the Avon is what many consider to be the jewel in Hampshire's crown, the New Forest. Originally established as a jealously-guarded hunting ground by King William nearly a thousand years ago, today it is the haunt of people, ponies and a huge range of wildlife and is equally jealously guarded for the unique qualities of its medieval landscape.

To attempt to describe the fascination of Hampshire in a few words or pictures is an all but impossible task, but it is hoped that this book will, at the very least, provide a flavour and prompt a greater exploration of this beautiful county at the advent of the new millennium.

The west front of Winchester cathedral

WINCHESTER AND THE CENTRAL CHALKLANDS

Overlooked by the statue of King Alfred the Great who made Winchester his capital, this beautiful medieval city, surrounding one of the finest cathedrals in Europe, is full of interest. The Great Hall, a remnant of the castle built by Henry III, housing the Arthurian round table; Wolvesey Castle, the ruins of the medieval Bishop's Palace; Winchester College, founded in 1382 and the oldest school in England and, best of all, the cathedral set in its peaceful close. To explore and marvel at its treasures and architecture is well worth while. But to visit on a frosty Winter evening to hear the soaring voices of the choir celebrating Christmas is an unforgettable experience.

Within the Close, the ancient Pilgrim Hall is now used by the Pilgrim School, whilst nearby the timber-framed houses of Cheyney Court next to one of the exits from the Close, Saint Swithun's Gate, are most picturesque. Just beyond and through the gateway is Kingsgate with Saint Swithun's church built above, which leads through the city walls and on to College Street.

To the south of the city and within an easy and enjoyable walk by the side of the sparkling waters of the River Itchen is Saint Cross Hospital. Built in 1136 by a grandson of William the Conqueror, to house thirteen poor men and provide daily food for others, it is still a tranquil retreat today. Nearby, but on the far side of the river, the fortifications of the Iron Age hillfort built on the top of Saint Catherine's Hill provide wonderful views of the city and surrounding countryside and, during the summer, the pleasure of flowers, butterflies and other insects as well.

To the east, the River Itchen flows by a series of pretty villages including Martyr Worthy, Itchen Abbas and Itchen Stoke until reaching New Alresford, a town once famous for its sheep fairs and originally founded by a Bishop of Winchester in 1199. The area is known for its extensive watercress beds and it is from here the steam trains of the restored Mid-Hants Railway, better known as the Watercress Line, regularly run.

Elsewhere in the area there is much to explore and enjoy, including the little green painted church in the wood built for use by gypsies camped nearby on Bramdean Common and the monument on the top of Farley Mount to a horse which survived a leap into a chalkpit and was subsequently renamed Beware Chalk Pit. From here it seems much of the county can be seen below, just waiting to be discovered.

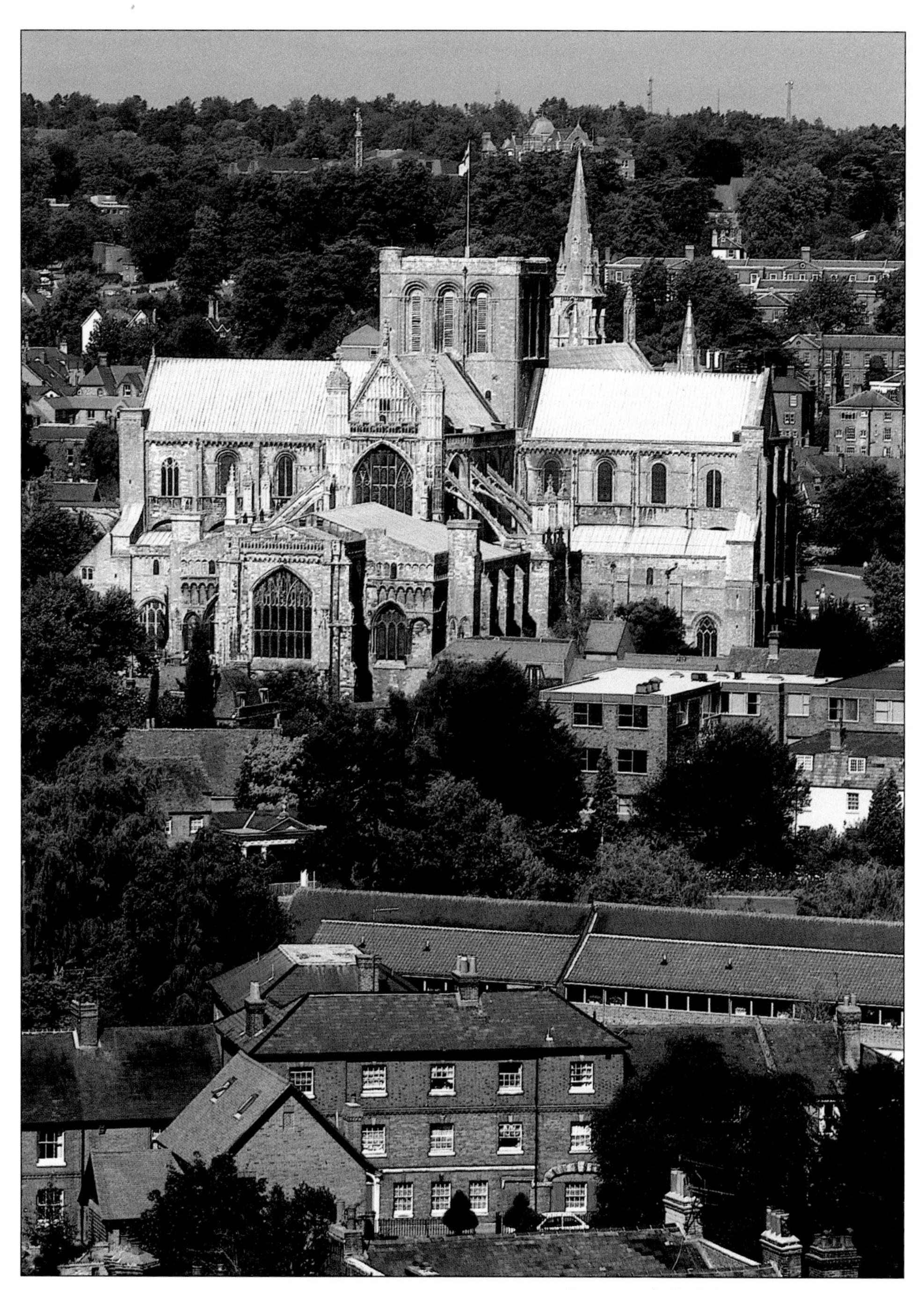

Winchester Cathedral from Saint Giles' Hill.

Cheyney Court, Winchester, formerly the Bishop's Court House.

Round table in the Great Hall, Winchester.

High Street, Winchester.

View from Farley Mount.

Farley Mount, a memorial to a brave horse.

Pond at Stoke Charity.

The Church in the Wood or the Iron Church, originally built for gypsies camping on Bramdean common.

The village pond at Crawley.

Saint Swithun's church, Martyr Worthy.

A school outing on Saint Catherine's Hill near Winchester.

Mill house on the River Itchen at Abbots Worthy.

Avington House near Itchen Abbas.

Cottage at Micheldever.

Saint Cross Hospital founded in 1136.

The lodgings for the brothers at Saint Cross Hospital.

Old fulling mill on the River Itchen at Alresford.

SOUTHAMPTON AND SOUTHAMPTON WATER

Although there is little to be seen of Roman Southampton (Clausentium) or of Saxon Southampton (Hamwic) other than in local museums, the medieval town is much in evidence despite wartime depredation and modern development. Much of the defensive walls and towers are still to be found. The West Gate, where the Mayflower left for America, and the adjacent Tudor Merchant's Store are both little changed. Whilst the impressive Bargate, still used by traffic until the 1930s, is now isolated near the town centre. Within the walls various old buildings survive including the Tudor House, Wool House, Medieval Merchant's House and an especially fine timber-framed house, now the Duke of Wellington pub.

Further south, along the east bank of Southampton Water, the River Itchen finally finishes its journey as does, a little further on, the River Hamble. Between the two are the remains of Netley Abbey, founded by monks from Beaulieu in the New Forest in 1239. Nearby is the Royal Victoria Country Park, once the site of a huge Army hospital, of which only the chapel now survives. Running for almost a mile along the edge of the Water, it is a popular place to visit.

At the mouth of the River Hamble is the village of Hamble on one side and Warsash opposite with the two joined by a ferry. There are marinas and moored yachts all the way upstream to Bursledon where, at a little distance, is an attractive old windmill.

On the west bank of Southampton Water, Hythe marina is a favourite spot to watch the great liners leaving port from the docks opposite. Even closer views can be obtained by walking or taking the tiny railway to the end of the seven hundred yards long Hythe pier where the ferry leaves for Southampton. Further south Ashlett Creek remains a haven of peace with just a pub, old tide mill and small collection of yachts.

At the mouth of Southampton Water, Calshot was once an RAF base for seaplanes and flying boats and the site of the Schneider Trophy air races between the wars. In 1931 the race was won for the third time by a locally built Supermarine, an aircraft ultimately developed into the Spitfire. Today, with marshes on one side of the spit and a colourful row of beach huts on the other, huge hangars now used as an activity centre and the old castle, one of many built by Henry VIII to protect the south coast, it is a strange mixture.

Container terminal at Southampton docks.

Ocean Village, Southampton.

QE2 *leaving Southampton.*

River Itchen from the Itchen Bridge, Southampton.

The Mayflower Memorial, Southampton.

Tudor Merchant's Hall and West Gate, Southampton.

Balloon Festival, Southampton.

Tudor gardens at the Tudor House Museum, Southampton.

Hampshire Farm Museum at Manor Farm near Botley.

Old hospital chapel, Royal Victoria Country Park near Netley.

Ruins of Netley Abbey.

Bursledon Marina.

Arcadia *passing Hythe Marina.*

Hythe ferry railway.

High Street, Hythe.

Bursledon windmill.

Chase Mill, Bishop's Waltham.

The old tide mill at Ashlett Creek.

Sailing on the Solent.

Bait digging on Lepe foreshore.

THE NEW FOREST AND SOUTH WEST COAST

Once a royal hunting ground, the New Forest is now one of the most visited areas in the country. Extending over some 93,000 acres it is a magical mix of heathlands, ancient woodlands, bogs and streams which together support a wonderful range of wildlife as well as some 7000 ponies, cattle and donkeys all owned by the local commoners.

Various villages are found in the Forest including Lyndhurst, the busy 'capital' and traditional centre of Forest activities. Beaulieu is at the tidal limit of the Beaulieu river and is popular not only for its attractive centre next to the river and picturesque mill pond, but also as the site of the National Motor Museum and remains of the once great monastery. At Buckler's Hard two rows of mellow, red-brick cottages face each other from either side of the wide green. With the yachts moored on the placid river below, it is hard to imagine that only two hundred years ago this peaceful scene echoed to the sound of workmen busily building wooden warships for the Royal Navy, including Nelson's 64 gun ship the *Agamemnon.*

On the far side of the river, although only accessible via Beaulieu by road, is Exbury Gardens with its delightful and internationally famous collection of rhododendrons and azaleas spread over 250 acres.

Lymington is found to the south of the Forest and is now best known as a yachting centre. The wide and busy High Street with its popular Saturday market leads down to the most attractive part of the town on the water front. Quay Hill, the quay itself and, close by, Captain's Row and Nelson Place with their small prettily painted houses, are all worth exploring. To the south of the town towards Keyhaven and Hurst Castle are the Pennington and Keyhaven marshes where the network of sea walls provides enjoyable walking in this wild and windswept area.

Ringwood is by the side of the River Avon and although much of the old town survives, including the busy Wednesday street market, parts have been replaced by modern development. Sadly this also brought to an end the old cattle market, a great loss to the surrounding area and especially the Forest.

Upstream, Fordingbridge is also by the river which is crossed at this point by a fine seven-arched medieval bridge. In the park next to the bridge is a striking statue of Augustus John, the painter, who lived nearby for a number of years. To the north, near Woodgreen, Castle Hill provides a wonderful view across the river and valley spread below.

Sunrise over the Beaulieu river at Beaulieu.

Buckler's Hard and the Beaulieu river.

Mill pond and Palace House at Beaulieu.

Kite flying at Bolton's Bench, Lyndhurst.

Thatching at Swan Green, Lyndhurst.

The Queen's House at Lyndhurst.

Lyndhurst old deer park near Matley.

Market day at Lymington.

Quay Hill, Lymington.

The quay at Lymington.

Lymington Quay.

Wilverley Plain, New Forest, in August.

Sunset over Wilverley Plain.

Lymington river, Brinken Wood, New Forest.

Boldre church.

Exbury Gardens in May.

Summer by the River Avon at Fordingbridge.

Martin church from Toyd Down.

Ringwood market.

Sea walls near Keyhaven.

Hurst Castle and light.

Mill Lawn Brook at Markway, New Forest.

River Avon and Breamore Mill from Castle Hill.

Dawn on the Lymington river in Brinken Wood, New Forest.

Withybed Bottom, New Forest.

Pigs at pannage in Denny Wood in the New Forest.

A cold, snowy day in the New Forest.

Warwickslade in the New Forest.

STOCKBRIDGE, ROMSEY AND THE LOWER TEST

Seeing the crystal clear waters of the Test on a sunny summer's day with flowers along its banks and overhung with trees here and there, it is all too easy to appreciate the delights of fly fishing. But with a rod on some of the river beats costing anything up to £300 per day, it can be an expensive pleasure.

Stockbridge is at the centre of some of the best trout fishing in the country and is well worth a visit. Falling somewhere between a large village and a small town, the single wide street spanning the river and various culverts is lined with a mix of handsome buildings and variety of shops. Reflecting the interests of the area, two of the shops are stocked with a great range of fly fishing essentials, whilst nearby at the Grosvenor Hotel is the base for the exclusive Houghton Club, the oldest fishing club in the country. To the south, a short stroll from the centre, Stockbridge Common is a pretty area running alongside the river.

Mottisfont Abbey is further along the Test valley to the south. Originally a priory established in 1200, it was converted into a house in the mid-1500s and has been much altered since. Parts of the house are now open to the public, but it is the grounds which are probably of greatest interest. Within the small park are some wonderful specimen trees and, near to the car park, a charming walk by the tree-lined banks of the Test. Best of all is the walled garden which houses the National Trust's extensive collection of old fashioned roses.

The attractive town of Romsey is also by the Test and although there has been much building on the outskirts, the centre remains compact and welcoming. Near the centre and doubtless partly responsible for the development of the town stood Romsey Abbey. Founded almost 1100 years ago it was once rich and powerful with influential royal connections. But this did not save it from being almost entirely destroyed in 1544 following the Dissolution of the Monasteries. The only part to survive was the church which was purchased by the town for £100. Today this lovely example of Norman architecture stands just a few paces from the Market Square where there is a statue of Lord Palmerston, former owner of Broadlands House which was later to become the home of Lord Mountbatten.

To the west is East Wellow where, in the churchyard, is the Nightingale family monument which includes the inscription 'FN 1820–1910', a modest memorial to the brave and selfless Florence Nightingale.

Florence Nightingale memorial, Saint Margaret's church, East Wellow.

River Test at Stockbridge.

Summer harvest near King's Somborne.

Romsey Abbey.

Town centre, Romsey.

Broadlands House, Romsey.

River Test near Mottisfont.

Old mill house on the River Anton at Fullerton.

Fly fishing on the Test at Leckford.

Walled garden at Mottisfont Abbey famed for its collection of historic roses.

ANDOVER, WHITCHURCH AND THE UPPER TEST

At one time Andover was an important medieval town and changed little until the 1960s when it was selected for development. The mass of new building for houses, commerce and industry together with new roads resulted in the loss of many of the older buildings. However, in the centre of the town Bridge Street, London Street and the High Street, overlooked by the Guildhall and the site of a Saturday street market, remain little altered. Nearby, the old Town Mill on the River Anton is a peaceful corner of an otherwise busy town.

To the west, the Thruxton motor racing circuit periodically roars into life, whilst speed of a quieter and more natural kind can be seen nearby at the flying displays of raptors which are regularly given by the Hawk Conservancy at Weyhill. Barely two miles away at Abbotts Ann, a different tradition still survives. Hanging just beneath the ceiling in the church are a series of maidens' garlands commemorating those who were born, baptised and confirmed in the parish but who died unmarried. An unusual and rather poignant sight.

Pretty villages such as Wherwell, with its white painted thatched cottages, and Longparish are found by the side of the Test which eventually leads on to Whitchurch. Here, on an island in the river, the silk mill still operates as it has done since 1830. Elsewhere, numerous Georgian buildings and a scattering of timber-framed houses together make this an attractive centre.

Joining the Test just below Whitchurch is the Bourne valley with chalk hills rising on either side. Here again there are a series of pretty villages seemingly little changed over the centuries. Hurstbourne Priors where the cricket pitch and thatched pavilion are overlooked by the church and stately trees, a most English scene. Saint Mary Bourne where the village seems to cluster tightly round the interesting twelfth-century church. Beyond, as the Bourne rivulet becomes more fickle, often disappearing for weeks at a time during the dry, hot days of summer, is Hurstbourne Tarrant, deep in the valley surrounded by hills.

Elsewhere it is all rolling countryside and small villages, much of which can best be appreciated from the top of Beacon Hill. Here, in addition to the wonderful sweeping views, is an Iron Age hillfort and the iron-railed grave of the Earl of Carnarvon, the discoverer of Tutankhamen, who lived close by at Highclere Castle which is just within sight to the north nestling among the trees.

View of Hurstbourne Tarrant.

Hawk Conservancy at Weyhill.

Cottage at Longparish.

Highclere Castle.

Estate cottages at Freefolk.

Village green, Ashmansworth.

Saint Peter Church, Linkenholt.

Monxton village

BASINGSTOKE AND THE NORTHERN BORDER

Basingstoke must be the only town in the county where the modern is more striking than the old. The town was designated for London overspill in the 1950s, and as a result much of the old town was destroyed in developing the large new elevated pedestrian centre. A few parts did escape including the lovely old Town Hall, now the Willis Museum, and the Deane Alms Houses dating from 1608 and still in use. But most eye-catching of all are the huge office buildings, all concrete and glass, strung along Churchill Way. A scene which almost seems alien in an otherwise largely rural county.

Old Basing is just to the east of the modern town and is perhaps best known for the seige of Basing House during the Civil War. This great house was built on the site of a Norman castle during the sixteenth century by William Paulet, an important and long serving employee of the Crown. And there is no doubt that it was not only the stubbornness of the defenders but also the difficulties caused by the old Norman defences that resulted in this being the longest seige of the war. After finally submitting, the house was burnt and raised to the ground leaving only the remains to be seen today.

The Basingstoke Canal, opened in 1798, meanders its rather tortuous route from the now partially collapsed Greywell Tunnel across the county boundary into Surrey and on to the River Wey. Narrowboat trips are available from Odiham, although low water levels during particularly dry summers can sometimes limit the distance available to the boats. There are also attractive canal side walks and, near Odiham, the chance to admire the formidable remains of Odiham Castle, built by King John in 1215.

In the north-east corner, the large expanse of Fleet Pond, set in a well wooded nature reserve, is popular with fishermen and bird-watchers alike. A little to the north is Yateley Common Country Park. Here, Wyndham's Pool, a pretty lake enjoyed by picnickers is surrounded by open heathland with scattered birch and pine reminiscent of the scenery to be found in the New Forest at the opposite end of the county.

By contrast, Wellington Country Park provides a mixture of attractions. Based on flooded gravel pits, boating and windsurfing are available together with rides on a model steam railway. There is also a small collection of farm animals for the children to enjoy and a large deer park with good herds of both red and fallow deer.

Red deer rutting at Wellington Country Park.

Basing House, Old Basing, a casualty of the Civil War.

Knot garden at Basing House, Old Basing.

Deane Alms Houses, Basingstoke, established in 1608.

A day out on the Basingstoke Canal.

Upton Grey.

Village post office, Kingsclere.

Mattingley church.

Remains of Odiham Castle built by King John in 1207.

Stables at Stratfield Saye House.

ALTON, PETERSFIELD AND THE WESTERN WEALD

Small market towns and villages, sometimes dramatic scenery and people whose names have survived the passing years, make this comparatively quiet and essentially rural area a pleasure to explore.

The market town of Alton has a good variety of buildings dating from a range of periods and an interesting museum displaying the long and varied history of the area. It was also here that a new phrase entered the English language, 'Sweet Fanny Adams', when, in 1867, an eight-year-old child of that name was cruelly murdered and is now buried in the local cemetery.

To the south, Chawton is a pretty village and birth place of Jane Austen. Whilst barely three miles to the east is Upper Froyle where the charm of many of the timber-framed houses, thatched cottages and other properties is enhanced by small statues of saints set in niches, the legacy of a former lord of the manor following his travels in Italy.

Further to the south, Isington Mill is beautifully situated on the River Wey and was formerly the home of Viscount Montgomery of Alamein who is buried nearby in a quiet corner of the churchyard at Binstead. Fame of a rather different kind is to be found at Bentley where the day-to-day lives of the villagers has been filmed over a long period for the popular television series 'The Village'.

Set in the more dramatic scenery of steeply rising hills and tree covered hangers is Selborne, birth place and home of Gilbert White the naturalist. His book *The Natural History of Selborne,* published over two hundred years ago, remains a popular classic and has been produced in countless editions. In addition to the attractions of the village and his house 'The Wakes', there are some wonderful walks in the area. Perhaps beyond the church and along the Oakhanger Stream and back through the woods or, for the more energetic, the climb up the zig-zag which was so laboriously constructed by White and his brother and which now provides glorious views of the village and surrounding countryside.

Petersfield, like so many other towns, has been unable to resist modern development. But here at least the Rams Walk development is varied and, although very close, has not destroyed the essential character of the town. The parish church still overlooks the Market Square where a statue of King William III surveys the scene. Elsewhere there is a great variety of interesting buildings including a Teddy Bear Museum to amuse the children.

East Meon.

The Square at Petersfield.

Market day at Alton.

Sunken track in Great Dorton Wood near Selborne.

Isington Mill near Binstead, previously the home of Viscount Montgomery of Alamein.

Jane Austen's House at Chawton.

Selborne and 'The Wakes', once home of Gilbert White, viewed from the zig-zag.

Medstead and Four Marks station on the Mid-Hants railway, better known as the Watercress Line.

The church is all that remains of the medieval village of Hartley Mauditt.

Statue of a saint, one of a number placed on estate houses by the lord of the manor at Upper Froyle.

Church of the Holy Cross, Binstead.

Village pond at Buriton.

PORTSMOUTH, FAREHAM AND THE MEON VALLEY

To many the name Pompey still conjures up visions of drunken sailors, a pub on every corner and a generally rough place. But this is no longer the case. Following the closure of the dockyard, new industries have arrived with tourism being among the most important. And although there are still many pubs to be found, there are also more museums in Portsmouth than practically anywhere else in the country.

The town first developed as a small port in the area today known as Old Portsmouth, at the entrance to Portsmouth Harbour, and it is here and along the Southsea front further south that the greatest range of interest for the visitor will be found.

The comings and goings of the ships, ferries and other craft can best be seen from the end of The Point and the Round Tower nearby, which are both situated at the narrow entrance to the harbour. *HMS Warrior*, the first ironclad warship, built in 1860, is found by the side of the Hard where the ferries leave for Gosport and boat trips round the harbour are available. *HMS Victory*, Nelson's ship at the battle of Trafalgar, is found in the old dockyard together with the surprisingly large remains of the *Mary Rose*. The ship sank in the Solent in 1545 before the doubtless horrified eyes of King Henry VIII and the captain's wife, and was eventually recovered in 1982.

Southsea is now a popular seaside resort where the D-Day Museum, Sea Life Centre, various naval memorials and other interest are to be found. Whilst at the top of Portsmouth Harbour is Portchester, best known for its near-complete Roman fort and medieval castle built inside. At Fareham there are a good number of fine old buildings together with attractive street scenes, although the once important quays have now declined due to silting.

Away from these busy centres, peaceful areas are still to be found along the coast such as Titchfield Haven and Langstone Harbour, both well known to bird-watchers. Inland, the old Forest of Bere area remains well wooded. Further north, Hambledon is one of the most picturesque villages in the county. Close by, modern cricket developed on the bleak, windswept and unlikely setting of Broadhalfpenny Down where Hambledon Cricket Club, once the most famous in the country, played from the mid-1700s. Today cricket is still played here next to the memorial to the original club and near the essential facilities of the Bat and Ball pub.

Southsea beach in Winter.

Portchester Castle.

The quay at Emsworth.

Road to the quay at Emsworth.

A day on the beach at Southsea.

HMS Warrior *at Portsmouth, the first ironclad warship.*

Boat trip to see the warships in Portsmouth harbour.

View from Bath Square, Portsmouth.

Ancient and modern – pubs on The Hard at Portsmouth.

Fareham Quay.

Langstone, once the haunt of smugglers.

Butser Ancient Farm near Petersfield.

All Saints' church, Catherington.

Mill Lane at Droxford.

Strawberry picking near Titchfield.

Saint Hubert's church at Idsworth.

Bird watchers at Farlington Marshes Nature Reserve.

View towards Old Winchester Hill.